GW0164453

The Girl whose Name I Never Knew
copyright © Keith Harris 2020
ISBN 978-1-903466-11-7

All rights reserved.
No part of this book may be reproduced in any
form without the permission in writing from both
the copyright owner and the publisher.

Cover illustration © Karen Horup Mathiasen

This book is published by ***Pending Press*** Ltd.

The Girl whose Name I Never Knew

Keith Harris

Published by **Pending Press** Ltd.

Who is one's neighbour ...? It is the being nearest to one at or since the beginning; this is one's sister soul for all eternity; this is one's twin soul, the soul together with whom one beheld the dawn of humankind.

(*Meditations on the Tarot*, Anon.)

Once I had a secret love

Preface

Should not a piece of writing stand by itself without need of an introduction? This is though a letter and the one to whom it is written will almost certainly never hold it in her hands.

As I write these words it is with a lingering sense of trepidation for this work is intensely autobiographical.

Its form can be compared to a diary. A diary written fifty years after the events began. The precise dates my memory no longer holds. The experiences, inner and outer, are riven with life almost as if they had occurred yesterday.

The co-creator of this writing is the girl whose name I never knew for without her these experiences would never have arisen. I write this to her yet ...

Imagine someone stranded on a desert island who writes a message to a long lost love, pops into a bottle and seals it with a kiss, er, I mean a cork. Watching sadly as it sails away tossing upon the waves, he realises the chance of it ever reaching her are infinitesimal.

If the bottle is plastic, the top tight and if no sharks gobble it up maybe it will be found by someone who reads it. Even then the chance of her ever receiving it are slimmer than the thickness of a spider's web.

This diary-letter is written to her, for her and cast out as it were onto the ocean waves in the hope it may be found and read by others, and that one of these readers might be able to place it into her hands.

Most readers will doubtless shake their heads at this clown of a writer. A few, who knows, might find an occasional echo of moments in their own lives.

Recently I related these events to some of my students. They were adamant they should be written down. No, I thought, it is too personal, raw and botched by my youthful inadequacy and absurdity to be believed. *You can't give up trying to find her,* they replied. No, I thought, no, it's close on half a century ago.

Less than a couple of weeks later, Christmas 2019, I began to write and felt there was meaning and purpose, perhaps even urgency to the task.

Prose with its stolid conventions isn't quite appropriate for the jotter form of a diary, neither is poetry with its air and aftermath of supra-personal meaning. I have employed the terseness and gimmickry of the line but blended this in places with normal sentences.

The text was written and revised between Christmas Eve 2019 and Epiphany 2020. Afterwards it was only slightly refined in a few places.

To you for whom this letter is written, I wish your life to have been blessed with deeply meaningful human relationships and fulfilment in your vocation (for some reason I believe you may have become a teacher of young children). Know this: I will never intrude in your life. If anyone has ever taught me unselfish love it is you.

More than anything I want to tell you how grateful I am that we met. I cannot envisage my life if we had never encountered each other. Some part of me would always have remained arcane and undisclosed. I experienced, even if only from afar, falling in love with the fairytale princess – a priceless treasure.

It is the nature of human life to love and lose. Whether of the widow whose husband dies in war, the parents whose child leaves and settles in a far-off country or the happy couple who find their lives drifting ever further apart. Life is more than finding the princess or the prince, we have so much to do in the search to follow our guiding star and to help our troubled world.

Yet is it not so that we must first learn to love one human being unselfishly and with all our heart that we can learn to love others with an echo of this same true love? And how can we love the beings we encounter in nature if we have not first learnt to love a human being?

* * *

This all begins in October 1969 at a disco for those who had just started at the university. I was eighteen and felt confident enough to ask a girl for a dance. Having had a bit of a thing about redheads, I saw one and thought I would ask her for a dance. She was sitting beside another girl with long light brown hair. I stood just behind them and said, *Er.*

The girls turned to look up at me. The girl with hazel hair gave me the loveliest smile anyone has ever given me. I have always remembered the enchanting quality of openness and immediacy in that smile. Semi-automatically though I asked the redhead for a dance. We danced, chatted, went out to a pub and parting for the evening agreed to meet up again. This was before mobile phones, there was a glitch we did not manage to meet up or make another date.

Though not completely certain, because I cannot properly picture her face, I think the girl, who gave me the beautiful smile, was the one to whom this is written. Three undergraduate years passed in which I have no memory of seeing her again.

To the Girl whose Name I Never Knew

I love you still though fifty
years have fled
since I first felt your presence
in the radiance of that
maiden smile
and asked the ginger-haired girl
sitting beside you for a
dance instead of you.

Three undergraduate years passed in Sheffield when I
hardly recall seeing you at all.

Commencing doctorate studies an
eager student of pure maths with
esoteric yearnings and my own
office in a Victorian town house and a
room in Vicky Flats, and, who knows,
a possible future in research.

One overclouded autumn afternoon
in a student union café my
medical-student mate pointed you out
muttering, *She's very sad, she's
been chucked by a graduating medic.*
And I remembered having seen you
somewhere before but
never witnessed such feminine
sorrowing nor such loveliness.

I had been enamoured with a librarian twice
my age who I even asked out but
nothing came of it. All that summer
after graduating she had been the centre
of my constant pining. After seeing you,
as a certain someone once said,
I have forgotten that name and that name's woe.
The librarian and all
other women disappeared.

A day or two later me and my math-grad mate, Bob,
played table football against you and another guy.

So often you wore a short
maroon jacket with your long
hint of a wave hazel hair
and living sad-eyed playful
loveliness.
That night I dreamt.
In dream walking, looking
earnestly for something I knew
not what. Suddenly you were
before me, clad in that maroon
coat, our arms opened and we
kissed. At our lips
first touch the world and all
its cares and chaos
vanished
only colourless, soundless
presence of universal being

samadhi-like and alive
not you, not me but wondrous
oneness: Sat, Chit, Ananda
Being, Consciousness, Bliss.
I awoke and wondered
what this might portend.

Next time I saw you, you
looked back at me as though our
dream kiss had been more
than mere mystic subjectivity.
Had we met and known
each other in the night?

You looked back at me
poignancy profound and piercing
in your luminous brown eyes
breaking down barriers between
two separated selves.

Bereft, some flotsam lost
in love, you
so beautiful and me
an ugly nondescript
with goofy teeth.

You a fairytale princess
and me no hero prince
just a chap who sensed an ocean-
wide gap between your beauty and
my insignificance.

A bloke who deemed his dick
to be too short to
make much impression.

It was easy, too easy
to down a few pints and stare
at you and simultaneously
into my makeshift self.

At nine o'clock the libraries closed
the union bar filled up.
I would wander in with a
pint or two inside me casting
about until I saw you. My
sight was like a light
tap upon your shoulder
a tactile arm you sensed
for in the instant I
noticed you, you would turn
around and look at me –
gazing
into each other,
seconds
passing still,
cradling
each other's glance –
until I unmanned
would turn away and down
another pint and wander
aimlessly into the street-lit
dark or wait and hope without
a sense of hope.

How many times this happened
if my memory hasn't multiplied
its number many, many times.
You might be chatting with a group
of friends, Hendrix's *Purple Haze* sounding
from the juke at near concert-level
decibels, yet in the moment when
my sight alighted on your hair you
turned around our eyes meeting,
two tactile arms embraced and time
was not ... till I
lost to myself purchased
another pint.

Once at closing time you
turned to me as we were leaving the
union bar and stopped as if
begging me to speak
I spoke
not
just stood there still
and stared.

But a few weeks after starting my PhD. studies your
ever-presence had settled inside me.

Days alone in my gas-fire heated
office gazing meaninglessly
out at grey sombre streets
seeing only reflections

of your face and figure vivid
in my mind, Maths
I couldn't meddle with.
Half an hour then a cup
of tea or coffee at the café
opposite the Hick's building listening
to jukebox vibes of *My Sweet
Lord* or *Killing Me Softly.* Back
to the office, time to kill
till the libraries closed
at nine o'clock.

Sometimes walking city streets
seeing a girl with long
your-coloured hair my
feet would follow hoping
it was you. Maybe
it never was.

Middle of the day wandering
Sheffield streets, without apparent
cause I would encounter
ecstasy – out
of myself, alive with harmony,
all life around infused and free
all was as it should be –
moments lasting many minutes while
meandering the city's roads.
The aftermath a course coming
down into a body which felt
as a bag of shite might feel.

(In case you're wondering
I never did no drugs
but even then I guess I was
allergic to alcohol.)

Esoteric longings, attempts
to make mine Ramana Maharishi's
meditative search: the
Who am I?
Questing for the higher self –
another self, female
with a shining I gently
infused
my spiritual strivings.
There was in truth
just no time for maths.

My young body bore its sexual
urge. Yet you were my fairytale –
how could I wank
with you in mind? (It happened
just the once.) Such drives
though are tough to
sublimate. In bed a quandary:
My heart wished only to
long for
you. The beast backed
by my loins wanted to
lunge into
somewhere else.
"Oh, let me get it

over with!" I pictured
some waitress and quickly
jerked it off so I could return
to your pristine feminine presence
in my mind. My
fairytale so near
so far from me.

Once I dreamt we were together I
was pumping proudly away on top
of you, my cock grown nigh
twice its length. A performance
impressive enough to have drawn
porn-star applauses. In this
gymnastic coupling I glanced down
at you, you were looking up
at me frowning with a
questioning expression as if
to say, "What the f-
are you up to?" And I forgot
all about screwing and clasped
you tenderly to my heart.

All my years even from as young as nine or ten my fantasy had conjured imaginary feats of rescuing the girl I fancied from bad persons, the damsel in distress from brigands.

Once, in dream not in
imagination, I was the
hero rescuing you, the girl

I'd always hoped to win.
Run, I shouted, thinking to hold
off the ruffians on my own.
You stayed bravely beside me.
I woke and wondered
what this may have meant.

Night after night at nine
o'clock in that crowded union
bar to Roberta Flack's *The First
Time Ever I Saw Your Face*
our eyes encountering across
that intractable gulf we call
the world. Even my absurd
and bashful twenty-one year old
self was incapable
of carrying this on.
I resolved to try
to ask you out.

Lunchtime in the union foyer,
a girly smirk exchanged
with a friend as you approached,
I stood my ground right
in your path only a yard
or two between us, my
mouth beginning to open when
a mate rushing up grabbed my
arm pulling me roughly away
saying, *It's time
for a game of chess.*

Another occasion in that L-shaped
union bar, you were fetching
drinks. I manoeuvred myself
in front of you and exclaimed
in a fairly loud voice, *Excuse me,*
meaning to continue *May I ask you
out* – or words with a similar meaning.
You took it to mean, *Excuse me,
do you mind getting out of my way!*
and sending me a sharp and irritated look
dodged past me. The moment
had gone. I stood
there. The moment gone.

All these events are so vivid in my memory though 47 years have since come and floated far away. There was a time in the café that same one where your sadness was pointed out to me.

You were alone
at a table reading a book
I had to act and sat
down diagonally opposite
and began to stammer
out about how deeply you had
affected me. You shot me
half a smile and went
on reading, your foot resting
on the chair beside me rotating
back and forth. My mouth
dried up. I needed to

drink and stood up asking, *Can I
get you a glass of water?* Why,
why, why, I ask myself now
as so very many times before, did I
not ask if you wanted tea or
coffee then we might have begun
to amicably chat as normal
people meeting might have done.
But no, I asked if you wanted
water and you shook your head.
I came back, you were still sitting
apparently absorbed
in the book, your foot still flipping
on the chair beside me back
and forth. I just sat
not knowing what
to do or what to say.
Did you not realise how beautiful
you were, how inadequate
and unworthy of you I felt?
I might have asked what
you were reading, a sentence
to break the ice. I only sat
so glum and empty –
purpose and meaning seeping
into a sense of hopelessness.
Only at the moment I stood
up to leave, did you glance at me
a touch of sorrow-filled anguish
in your eyes. Head down
I walked sadly away.

What was I meant to do?
What was I? Who was I?
For what purpose was I living?
One night more drunk than
usual I made a decision
I would away to India to become
a beggar monk devoted solely
to the spiritual quest. I walked
a long way through dark
city streets and threw
my wallet, coins and keys
onto rooftops. Poverty
would accompany my hitch-hiking
to Holy India.
At the motorway junction holding
out my thumb but no one stopped
so I walked down the hard
shoulder, thumb still raised.
Cars droned past until
I got picked up
by the police. They could've
done me. They only laughed
at my meagre motivation to be
a yogi, took me back
to Vicky Flats suggesting
I sleep it off.

Then came the dialogue
with God – more like a moaning
monologue to my angel.

This part is tough to describe, hard to believe, difficult to explain even to myself but it did really happen.

> I had begun to wonder if
> I could get it up. Not good
> looking, a dick I'd never
> boast about and now
> possible impotence. A sad case
> of too many pints perhaps
> or was it just soft
> to picture some plump and pimply
> barmaid as a jerk-off image when
> I yearned to be with you. I tried
> to bargain with God. I
> imagined myself transformed, a
> handsomely potent male.
> And fantasised
> it might magically come
> about within a moment.

At the time I had a habit of tossing a coin when facing a choice. Heads or tails – heads usually reserved for the sensible alternative.

> A night came, doubtless
> I'd downed pints, surely
> I had seen you and sobbed
> inwardly at the abyss
> gaping between us. I wanted to force

God to choose: Transform
me or let me fall
to death. This night when angels
and demons must have surged
about me in troubling proximity.
Blocks of concrete council flats
at that time had no locks
on outer doors. I climbed the
concrete stairs of a concrete
block of council flats intent
on forcing God's hand: A frog
blessed by an angel's kiss
metamorphosing my body to a
prince's worthy of a fair princess.
Or an amphibian lying
squashed and bloody on the pavement
far below. I opened a window
on the stairs and looked
out, five or six storeys up,
it was a long way down. Dark,
dank, no fairytale atmosphere
suffused those concrete steps.
Was I
to jump or not to jump?
Were angels preparing a magical
metamorphosis? Some vague
hope had lingered as I in carefree
careworn drunken mood
had climbed those concrete stairs
now looking down, my imagined
sense of marvel sorely missing. Only

murky empty city streets. I
stood there questioning and took
the easy way out. You've guessed:
Heads or tails. Heads
the sensible decision: Walk
back down the stairs. Tails:
Fly out into airy darkness.
The coin clinked on the concrete.
I picked it up:
Tails.
And walked over
to the window. It was
a long way down. No sense
of rightness or of wrongness resided
in me. Was it only cowardliness
to trudge back down the steps?
No answer came toward me, no
answer rose inside. Again I
took the easy route and tossed
the coin. Once more I picked it up.
This time it was … tails again.
I trod heavily toward the open
window. No inkling of an answer
in my heart. Outside the night
was in no counselling mood. I saw
my body lying dead
and broken far below. I prayed,
got on my knees prayed and
promised this third time
counts for all. Tails
and I would fling myself

out into the unknown night.
The coin clinked on the concrete.
It was heads.

Walking back down the concrete steps no sense of relief arose. Courage, which hitherto I had never doubted I possessed, even that I lacked. Home to bed. But now I knew only one path was left: India and the yogi call, to renounce everything for the spiritual quest.

Looking back today I dare not even dare to think what may have taken place had the coin that third time shown tails.

> An only child. pocket
> money saved, still got enough
> for ice cream and chocolate.
> Popping coins into a money
> box through years of growing up
> all deposited in a bank
> account. I blew most of it on a
> one-way ticket to India.

When I told my mom and dad they sobbed. Their only child to be an outcast for the spirit far in the East. They cried and begged. I stepped back, promising just to take a holiday then to return and complete my PhD. They brought me a return ticket. Three and a half months in Holy India. A respite I could not have gone on without. Adventure, well after a fashion. The journey over was weird. My first trip outside of Britain. Change in Zurich, refuel in the Middle East, up to Karachi, down to Colombo, on to Bangkok, change again to Calcutta. The plane from Zurich, which I should have got, had been hijacked. One night in a posh hotel. Next morning's flight. Two days to Bangkok. I arrived with a ticket to Calcutta for the day before. It was my first trip outside of the UK. I could go on. The last train from Calcutta station before the strike. A crowded compartment. I arrived in Madras (Chennai) with a skin infection only saved by Aurovedic soap. Bus to Tiruvannamalai, Ramana Maharishi's ashram, the holy mount of Arunachala. He had died the year before I was born. No resident guru only a quality of peace in the meditation halls.

Three and a half months in India, you were with me, how could you not have been? Yet in and around the ashram an intimate quiet-filled urgency for the holy quest reigned, people to meet and chat to. The sheer intensity of my time in Sheffield drifted into the background.

Today I realise I was split apart. Two yearnings had ever resided in me. The hope of winning the princess and a longing deep inside to follow the holy, one might even say, grail quest. During my time in India I learnt again what I had always known. Romantic love and the quest for genuine spiritual progress are entirely compatible. India was a time of restful hope.

Returning to Sheffield and taking up again my

studies, this lasted a month not more. At first I kept away from that L-shaped union bar. Until one evening in there with a pint. I spoke to some of Bob's mates by the bar and then sat down. You were there and came straight up to Bob's same mates chatting animatedly to them. From the far end of the place I watched and wondered what this meant and if any hope was left.

> The maths meant nothing.
> The beautiful time in India
> evaporated. I was in Sheffield
> stranded and in love. The
> circle continued, pints
> and meeting eyes. An I naked
> before an I – and hopeless
> unsettling aspirations.

> Did you know how much I
> loved you? I think
> maybe you did. Was my love
> requited or unrequited?
> Still I do not know. How could
> we never have spoken, never
> broken the ice. For me I think I
> might have needed a huge
> pneumatic drill to crack
> that icy cover separating us.
> From you one word
> would have melted an iceberg.

It was another time. Now it seems simply absurd. Could we not have spoken just the once?

> Every glancing exchange,
> a stepping into a shrine
> with holy awe, the touch
> of eternal higher selves.
> Our earthly persons destined
> never to embrace?

An outsider reading this probably assumes it was all my youthful fantasy. That I meant not a fig to you, that if you were ever to read these pages you would probably not even remember the bloke whose heart was broken open whenever he looked at you.

As once again I rekindle in living memory our glances I know this is not so. I did mean something to you. How deep this was for you that I do not know.

Have you forgotten me?

A few years after leaving Sheffield I read Dante's *La Vita Nova* about his experiences with Beatrice – and thought I was reading about myself.

The final curtain on my time at university nears. A sad close. My mate Bob believed his memory was like a box of limited space: pop something in and something already in pops out. Consequently he deemed everything inessential best forgotten. When we played table football he knew your name. But that was before our dream embrace and the kiss causing the world to disappear, before I realised I loved you.

When I asked him later about the name of the girl we played table football with … his memory was blank. Consequently I never discovered your name.

Maybe I had caught a glimpse of your true name but the name by which you are known I do not know.

A couple of times after leaving I even hitch-hiked back to Sheffield and the union bar. You were not there.

Many times I have thought about trying to trace the girl whose name I never knew. Every such thought only left an emptiness. If I had been able to trace you – a happily married woman maybe with three kids. I would have walked quietly away wishing you well with all my heart. But what purpose would that have served either for you or for me?

Life and destiny have not brought us together again. I have never met anyone who might have known you.*

In truth I do not know if you still live.

Though rosy lips and cheeks within his bending sickle's compass come … are we not all time's fools? I know if I were to meet you today your unbelievable physical beauty would be diminished. Would I know you? I know the I who looked through your brown eyes. However faded you might have become would not matter to me.

Destiny allowed us to meet but not to share our lives together.

For having met you I am truly grateful even

though the pain that pierced me then only raw physical hurt can outweigh.

> Who is able to rekindle
> hurt borne by a once experienced
> physical pain? I am not.
> I remember having had toothache
> but in this memory the
> ache is absent. Arrows piercing
> the psyche long years gone,
> in recalling those moments the
> hurt may live almost as acutely
> as when their shafts first tore into
> my tenderly opening heart.

What troubles me most even to this day is that I did not speak. Norms and perceived or imagined inadequacies plagued my young self. This has left inside me some blockage in the base of my psyche, a stone weighing down my heart or an open wound from where my life's blood quietly trickles away. Maybe both, a stricture and a seeping sore.

Late November, I think, in that second year of PhD studies (though the maths was light years distant). I was pretty drunk in the union bar. You as ever were with friends.

I said in a very loud voice, *Now I am really drunk!* and went up to you crassly begging for a date, *Will you go out with me?*

You embarrassed glanced at your friends and answered, *No.*

I asked you one last question, *Maybe another time?*

Again you answered, *No.*

Had I brought on a situation where your only reasonable choice was to say, *No* – or did you really mean it? I do not know, I do not know.

The remainder of that night was farce. I had been talking to a guy who had lived three doors down from me in our Vicky Flat. I ended up going to a disco with him, my one aim to get totally drunk. In that aim at least I succeeded. After leaving the disco he ordered a taxi and took me back to his flat. There he took off my shoes and pulled my trousers down, which even to my drunken mind felt odd. He helped me into his bed and lay down beside me. I felt his hand upon my knee. He drew it slowly toward my crotch.

In my state if someone had pointed a gun at my head and ordered me to get up I think I might have given them the middle finger and told them to get stuffed. But this, this – after just losing my fairytale princess – was more than a mote too much. I leapt out of bed, got dressed and got out of the building. Empty streets in a district of the city I did not know. Tiredness and drunken stupor returned. I milled about talking to myself not knowing where I was or where to go. And got picked up. This time the police were not so friendly. They took me to the cells.

I woke up on a hard wooden bench, a pair of stockinged feet near to my nose. I glanced down at my own feet, the head of someone else close to them.

I looked down at the floor, and if I remember aright, a pile of puke lay there. In the cell's corner was a toilet. At least I could piss. They came early to wake us. Tea and bread and jam for breakfast. One by one we were lead into the Magistrates Court.

My turn came. I stood on some sort of balcony at the back of the court. The police were witnessing against me. No doubt I had been drunk but had I been disorderly?

I heard the officer pronounce in solemn voice, *And he was suggesting that we did not have fathers.*

The female magistrate, probably in her early thirties, glanced up at me suppressing a smirk.

I had nothing to say for myself. She gave me the minimum fine and I was let out.

The worst night of my life had ended.

Only once more did we meet. That same day or maybe a day later I walked through the union bar, you were there with friends. One last sad glance and head lowered I passed by and out of your life.

You have ever remained in mine.

I bought a tent, a sleeping bag and hitch-hiked to North Wales. Camping out near Bedgelert on frozen ground in the Snowdonian mountain range. Desperately and unsuccessfully seeking to sublimate romantic love into a spiritual quest.

At Christmas I returned to my parents and my childhood home. A desperately low point in my life. My mate, Pete, saved me. He gave me a copy of *The Hobbit* as a Christmas present. When I was eleven our class teacher read to us from it every Friday afternoon for a couple of months. She read half of this wonderful book. I had never finished it. After getting through Pete's present I bought *Lord of the Rings* the day after Boxing Day. I read day and night, and even though being a slow reader, I managed to finish it in three days. This book changed my view of nature. A quality of rosy ethereal light reminiscent of an elven dawn suffused the trees and living growing things as I gazed at twilit nature. For a little while I lived more in the Middle Earth than in our troubled civilisation. This book, as my time in India, became a sacred respite.

No point keeping on with the lie of pretending to do maths. I dropped out of university. I still had though a room in a flat in Sheffield, my intention was to live there and go on the dole. Somehow I couldn't face the idea of leaving the city and never seeing you again. Early in 1974 I took a holiday walking in the Lake District and staying in youth hostels. Hardly any other guests were there but at one hostel an outward bound school was staying. Two women teachers and a group of youngsters. Pat, one of the teachers, was so like you. She might have been your twin only five or six years older with fair hair and blue eyes. If I had never met you …

She liked me too, I think, because she asked me if I wanted to be a driver at their school. My heart was sorely troubled, she looked so like you. Two days in the hostel, playing cards in the evenings and still I have a picture of her enshrined in my heart. She was so like you but she was not you.

My intention had been to hitch-hike back to Sheffield. I got a lift from some guy driving down to London passing near Birmingham and the Black Country where my parents lived. I thought I would return to my childhood home for a few days.

A few days became a week, a week two. The thought of returning to Sheffield and the piercing stab of seeing you … somehow I couldn't face. I allowed my ties to Sheffield to be severed. The nadir of my life was reached.

Forty six years have passed by since then. Somehow I feel a sense of urgency in writing this letter to you. I can't leave off here but equally I can't write an autobiography. There is something I need to explain, though whether for you or for myself I am not sure.

Since before I was ten, I had always been in love. Some schoolgirl in my class perhaps. Half a year maybe more and suddenly my romantic longings slipped onto another girl. For me, both then and now, this was a yearning for the fairytale princess.

So often I imagined scoring winning goals at Wembley, not to gain acclaim only to impress the girl my heart so hoped to win. In Sheffield you were there, the fairytale I had always longed for.

After this there was no fairytale to seek.

But there were still women. In a convoluted way this made it easier to fall in love because I never had to ask myself: *Is she the one?* You were the One … and you were gone.

I lived an intransient dichotomy. The princess and heavenly romance were lost to me, here below were only possibilities of earthly engagements or enticements.

Twenty eight and still a virgin. Thirty before I had my first real girlfriend, Grete in Norway. I need to tell you of a vivid dream. I dreamt I was marrying Grete. As I walked up the aisle all the friends I had ever known were there packed into the church. As we were walking back down the aisle again after marrying, you were suddenly before me. I stood looking at you in tears as if to ask, *Why, why now?*

You smiled so open-heartedly, waved and disappeared into the crowded congregation.

I awoke and felt you had given me leave to espouse Grete.

Grete broke it off again after a few months at Christmastide. (Christmas has so often been a bad time for me with women.)

I made a promise to myself that if ever I were to fall for someone I would not remain silent, I would at least speak to the girl. This promise, with one single exception, I believe I have kept. On a few occasions though it has led me into awkward situations.

So many women to have fallen for, mainly from a distance though a few did become girlfriends yet ... always the princess of my heart was you. Never a day passed without me vividly picturing you in my heart and mind. Almost thirty years, then early in 2003 I thought to myself, there is something different. I realised a week maybe more had gone by without me thinking about you. I had never made any effort to keep you in my mind, you were always there. Suddenly you were not there. I wondered if perhaps you were no longer living in this world.

Autumn 2003, a girl was looking at me with a depth and immediacy I had only once before encountered. Falling in love – and you were not there to save me! And as with you, thousands of times each day she vividly entered my mind. My feelings were not reciprocated. She was very much younger than me with a loveliness almost to rival yours. This falling in love cost me nine years of my life. Sometimes I wondered if she were not my little sister, the sibling my mother miscarried. If this sister had lived, she might have visited me in Sheffield … and maybe helped me break the ice between us, allowing us to speak to each other.

Wonderful though it might have been to have shared my life with you, I realise well enough I would not have been able to clean up so much of my karmic baggage. A great part of my life, especially the romantic entanglements with women, feels as though it were a healing of karmic trespassing, a repaying of karmic debt.

So many women who have wandered into my heart

and mind, now I only have a fondness for them all. Maybe the one true relationship we can take with us from earth to heaven is friendship.

At the end of my life I hope I can meaningfully repeat Anne Catherine's words, *I have nothing to forgive any living being.*

Of all these many women one stands out because this was not a distant or imagined relationship. It was full of genuine affection and very many earthly concerns and tasks. Pia, the mother of my children. We were together for ten years and have been heartfelt friends ever since. Today she is remarried, well the 're' is redundant since technically we never tied the knot.

Recently you have come again into my heart and mind as once you did with my twenty-one year-old self. Now though I carry on quietly with my life. What hope really do I have that we shall ever meet again? For although you might recognise yourself in this writing even your close friends are unlikely to grasp that the girl, whose name I never knew, is you.

This last summer taking a two-day break in Cornwall, an inkling arose in me that we might meet. Sadly no. Though a woman, with grey hair who might have been around my age, did catch my eye on the platform in Bristol where my train had stopped. She was walking up and down as if waiting for something or someone but she was too far away for me to see the I shining through her eyes, the chance of her being you infinitesimal. Nevertheless this was an important encounter for me. It brought home to me the fact that age brings about significant physical changes. Outwardly you will look different from the twenty-two year-old I can still picture so vividly.

Love is not love
which alters when it alteration finds
or bends with the remover to remove.

That I have never been able to meet you again, never been able to wish you well and ask for forgiveness for not having found the courage to speak to you when at university. This has left some part of me crippled, a knot tight around my heart. I feel unable to take the next step in my life unless I can discover who you are and wish you well. Or, if by some sad chance you no longer live in this world, to kneel and whisper a quiet prayer at your gravestone.

No, I realise I have to go on with my life, to do that which I have to do ... though the ache of never having known your name will linger with me to my dying day.

I need you to realise that I loved and love you so dearly that I cannot but help to love all those who have loved you ... be they children, friends or lovers.
May life have brought you many blessings.

This letter is but a message placed as it were in an imaginary bottle and tossed into the sea in the faint hope that someone who knows you may find and pass it on to you.

I love you
I love you still
I love you as the
angels love you.

* Footnote
In re-reading this draft I realised that this is not entirely correct. Some years after leaving Sheffield I made an effort to find Bob and succeeded. I visited him and asked if he or if his mates, to whom you had once spoken so animatedly, were able to remember anything about you ... blank again!

The ginger-haired girl, who I had danced with and spent an evening chatting to at my university start, I had also bumped into and exchanged a few friendly words with on about four or five occasions during our time as undergraduates. And I remembered her name. In the autumn of 1998 I was living in North Wales near Snowdonia and came across a scenic watercolour painted by someone with her name. I briefly visited the artist and her husband. She was indeed the ginger-haired girl I had known in Sheffield. She did not remember anything about me, why should she, more than a quarter of a century had elapsed since she graduated. When I hesitantly tried to explain about once asking her for a dance when she was sitting beside a girl who gave me a beautiful smile and who might have been the love of my life though I had never managed to discover her name ... I think she and her husband quietly concluded I must have been some sort of nutter.

What can I say? About you, my nameless princess, I have always been completely nuts.

In 2012 I went to a black-tie dinner in Sheffield for those of us who had graduated forty years before. You were not there. I mumbled to some of the girls who were working at the university about the possibility of finding a girl who had graduated about the same time as me. The answer: If you can tell us her full name, which subject(s) she graduated in and the year of her graduation then we can begin to talk about it.

What can I say? Maybe I need a miracle to find you.

Postscript

After re-reading the text I pondered again the meaning of you standing 'bravely beside me' in one of those vividly real dreams. It began to dawn on me that there was a depth in this image which I had not previously grasped.

Though this was not fully conscious during my time at university, it seems that like a fairytale prince I felt I had to achieve deeds, perhaps great deeds to win the princess. I felt somewhere deep inside me a need to do something special or to be someone special in order to be worthy of you. I saw myself as not good looking, as no super lover, whereas you were so extraordinary beautiful, a true fairytale princess. A princess I was hardly worthy of.

Is not the meaning of the image of you standing by me in the dream that I did not need to achieve anything nor did my earthly person have to be in some way elevated to win your heart? Maybe you would have loved me anyway for who I am and stood by me even in adversity. It has taken me 47 years to become aware of this possible meaning etched into that image. I am so deeply sorry that I did not realise and trust in this possible significance of the dream.

Today I seek to find an image of you which catches that which you are and which remains undiminished by time and ageing. In the words of Solomon from the Song of Songs:

for love is as strong as death, its flashes
are flashes of fire, a flame of the eternal.

Afterword

I would like to thank my mates who have listened to my sob stories over the years especially to Pepino, Gordone, Daffy, Roberto, Pellone, Kazino and the brothers Anderone and Mortone, also my parents and my kids for being there.

As vividly and as accurately as my memory has allowed I have sought to write about the things concerning you, the girl whose name I never knew. You have been a vital part of my life. Other essential aspects of my life I have hardly touched upon. I did mention the spiritual quest, the wish to know and to follow a path leading to life's true purposes which since my early teens has always been present in me. I have learnt that the higher quest and romantic love are genuinely compatible.

Something else began to stir in my depths after returning from India. This was the need to bring spiritual knowledge into life for the good of all humankind and for suffering nature. In a library a year or two after leaving university I came across a book about Steiner education. Here esoteric knowledge which I had long been aware of, such as that relating to the etheric and astral bodies, was brought into deeply meaningful pedagogical expression.

Ramana Maharishi, as I have already mentioned, was a vitally important figure in my life. And though I have never met them in person, Rudolf Steiner,

Valentin Tomberg and Anne Catherine Emmerich have been my revered and wonderful teachers.

Yet as ever was and ever will be Jesus Christ is my one and only guru. May Mary, His mother and ours, forever bless you, the girl whose name I never knew.

Now I shouted from highest hills
Even told the golden daffodils.
    (from the song: *Once I had a Secret Love*)

Not having left the train, to find out for certain whether the grey-haired woman I saw on the platform in Bristol might possibly have been the one this book is written for, has troubled me since the summer. Most especially because I had had an inkling that by some strange starlit chance we might have met in the little holiday break to the Cornish West.

In the first week of February 2020, as a kind of belated response to my inability to act upon that semi-slumbering intuition, I wrote the following poem, ***Waiting***.

Waiting

Walking on a platform up
and down, waiting,
waiting for somebody or for
a train to take you far
from where you stand?
Resolute impatience in your stride,
no baggage to be seen,
are you not there
therefore to meet someone; a
slightly anxious quality imbues
your presence, a person precious
to you then: a grandchild,
son or daughter, a friend
from far away or perhaps an
old and half-forgotten flame.

Your grey hair less
than shoulder length
and wide brown eyes
too distant for me to ascertain
who you really are.
You remind me of a girl I
knew many, many years gone.
Would she look as you look
now – with her hazel hair shorn
of colour and cut so short?
Is your face lined with love's
and lost love's poignant, palpitating
essences, etched with memories buoyant,
blemished or suppressed?

Worried determination exuding
from your steps as you wait
upon the concrete platform for
I know not who?
Why are you waiting? For life
to bring fresh meaning to a time
wasted in your student years –
as once I wasted mine
and missed the one my youth so
eagerly, earnestly, so longingly
had awaited … and so sadly lost.
Am I waiting for her still?
I hope life knows for I
know not.

A partition scythed
into my living psyche.
I have searched so many
female eyes in cafés, concerts,
peopled city streets, looking,
ever looking for one to heal
this softly bleeding cleft
shelved deep inside my cloven
solitude.
Midst life's constantly recurring
actions a lost-child cry
echoes from my heart calling, calling
silently into the silence
of a clouded dark-night sky.
I know stars still shine
alas I see them not.

My train is waiting.
It should have trundled
from the station many minutes
earlier. Should I leave
this crowded compartment, the company
of my grown-up kids and risk
missing its departure to wander
over to the other platform where
you wait
to find out if you
are her
or not?
If you are her – though I
know, as every grown-up knows,
such a fate-filled starlit cross of paths
in all probability is impossible.

The grey-haired woman on the platform
pads up and down. Inexorably my train
pulls out. The moment
departs. The chance,
so infinitesimal, has
passed me by.

In student years in the city where
we lived sometimes almost against
my will I would follow a girl with long
your-coloured hair, hoping
it was you. It never was.
What chance was there then
you were that waiting white-haired woman?

Yet now I wish I had reacted as an
adolescent trusting
in destiny and left
that overfilled compartment and my
adult self behind
to look her
in the I.

Are not moments of destiny as
improbable as the lamb sleeping
contentedly beside the lion?

From this bypassed encounter one tot
of comfort remains: the unbelievably
beautiful twenty-two year-old you were
retains her loveliness
for me
though once hazel hair
is hoary, though wrinkles crease
her cheeks and stiffness hamper
grace-filled movements of her limbs.
I love you still.

Absurdly implausible as it seems
I wish I knew for certain
whether the grey-haired woman
was you –
and whether she had
in some sense trusted
providence and allowed her feet
to arrive upon the platform at

that very hour
to wait impatiently
for me.